HOCKEY

PAUL ROMANUK

2009-2010

SUPERSTARS

Your complete guide to the 2009–2010 season,
featuring action photos of
your favorite players

SCHOLASTIC

THE TEAMS

ATLANTIC DIVISION

NEW JERSEY DEVILS
team colors: red, black and white
home arena: Prudential Center
mascot: N.J. Devil
Stanley Cups won: 3

NEW YORK ISLANDERS
nickname: Isles
team colors: orange, blue, white, silver and green
home arena: Nassau Veterans Memorial Coliseum
mascot: Sparky the Dragon
Stanley Cups won: 4

NEW YORK RANGERS
nickname: Blueshirts
team colors: blue, white and red
home arena: Madison Square Garden
Stanley Cups won: 4

PHILADELPHIA FLYERS
team colors: orange, white and black
home arena: Wachovia Center
Stanley Cups won: 2

PITTSBURGH PENGUINS
nickname: Pens
team colors: black, gold and white
home arena: Mellon Arena
mascot: Iceburgh
Stanley Cups won: 3

NORTHEAST DIVISION

BOSTON BRUINS
nickname: Bs
team colors: gold, black and white
home arena: TD Banknorth Garden
mascot: Blades the Bruin
Stanley Cups won: 5

BUFFALO SABRES
team colors: black, white, red, gray and silver
home arena: HSBC Arena
mascot: Sabretooth

MONTREAL CANADIENS
nickname: Habs
team colors: red, blue and white
home arena: Bell Centre
mascot: Youppi
Stanley Cups won: 24

OTTAWA SENATORS
nickname: Sens
team colors: black, red and gold
home arena: Scotiabank Place
mascot: Spartacat
Stanley Cups won: 7 (pre-1934 team)

TORONTO MAPLE LEAFS
nickname: Leafs
team colors: blue and white
home arena: Air Canada Centre
mascot: Carlton the Bear
Stanley Cups won: 11

SOUTHEAST DIVISION

ATLANTA THRASHERS
team colors: navy blue, light blue, orange, gold and red
home arena: Philips Arena
mascot: Thrash

CAROLINA HURRICANES
nickname: Canes
team colors: red, black and white
home arena: RBC Center
mascot: Stormy the Ice Hog
Stanley Cups won: 1

FLORIDA PANTHERS
nickname: Cats
team colors: red, navy blue, yellow and gold
home arena: BankAtlantic Center
mascot: Stanley C. Panther

TAMPA BAY LIGHTNING
nickname: Bolts
team colors: blue, black, silver and white
home arena: St. Pete Times Forum
mascot: ThunderBug
Stanley Cups won: 1

WASHINGTON CAPITALS
nickname: Caps
team colors: blue, black, gold and white
home arena: Verizon Center
mascot: Slapshot

EASTERN CONFERENCE

CENTRAL DIVISION

CHICAGO BLACKHAWKS
nickname: Hawks
team colors: red, black and white
home arena: United Center
mascot: Tommy Hawk
Stanley Cups won: 3

COLUMBUS BLUE JACKETS
nickname: Jackets
team colors: blue, red and green
home arena: Nationwide Arena
mascot: Stinger

DETROIT RED WINGS
nickname: Wings
team colors: red and white
home arena: Joe Louis Arena
mascot (unofficial): Al the octopus
Stanley Cups won: 11

NASHVILLE PREDATORS
nickname: Preds
team colors: navy blue, silver, white and gold
home arena: Sommet Center
mascot: Gnash

ST. LOUIS BLUES
team colors: white, navy blue and gold
home arena: Scottrade Center

NORTHWEST DIVISION

CALGARY FLAMES
team colors: red, gold, black and white
home arena: Pengrowth Saddledome
mascot: Harvey the Hound
Stanley Cups won: 1

COLORADO AVALANCHE
nickname: Avs
team colors: burgundy, silver, black and blue
home arena: Pepsi Center
Stanley Cups won: 2

EDMONTON OILERS
team colors: white, navy blue, orange and red
home arena: Rexall Place
Stanley Cups won: 5

MINNESOTA WILD
team colors: red, green, gold and wheat
home arena: Xcel Energy Center

VANCOUVER CANUCKS
team colors: blue, silver, red and white
home arena: General Motors Place
mascot: Fin

PACIFIC DIVISION

ANAHEIM DUCKS
nickname: Ducks
team colors: purple, green, silver and white
home arena: Honda Center
mascot: Wild Wing
Stanley Cups won: 1

DALLAS STARS
team colors: green, white, black and gold
home arena: American Airlines Center
Stanley Cups won: 1

LOS ANGELES KINGS
team colors: purple, white, black and silver
home arena: STAPLES Center

PHOENIX COYOTES
team colors: red, green, sand, sienna and purple
home arena: Jobing.com Arena
mascot: Howler

SAN JOSE SHARKS
team colors: teal, gray, orange and black
home arena: HP Pavilion
mascot: S.J. Sharkie

WESTERN CONFERENCE

YOUR FAVORITE TEAM

Name of your favorite team: _____

Conference and division: _____

Players on your favorite team at the start of the season:

Number	Name	Position
_____	_____	_____
_____	_____	_____
_____	_____	_____
_____	_____	_____
_____	_____	_____
_____	_____	_____
_____	_____	_____
_____	_____	_____
_____	_____	_____
_____	_____	_____
_____	_____	_____
_____	_____	_____
_____	_____	_____
_____	_____	_____
_____	_____	_____
_____	_____	_____
_____	_____	_____
_____	_____	_____
_____	_____	_____
_____	_____	_____
_____	_____	_____
_____	_____	_____
_____	_____	_____
_____	_____	_____

Changes, Trades, New Players

_____   _____   _____
_____   _____   _____
_____   _____   _____
_____   _____   _____
_____   _____   _____
_____   _____   _____
_____   _____   _____
_____   _____   _____

End-of-Season Standings

Fill in the name of the team you think will finish in first place in each of the six NHL Divisions.

EASTERN CONFERENCE

ATLANTIC DIVISION
NORTHEAST DIVISION
SOUTHEAST DIVISION

_____

_____

_____

CENTRAL DIVISION
NORTHWEST DIVISION
PACIFIC DIVISION

WESTERN CONFERENCE

_____

_____

_____

The Playoffs

Which two teams will meet in the Stanley Cup Final? Fill in their names below, then circle the team you think will win.

Eastern Conference Winner: _____

Western Conference Winner: _____

YOUR FAVORITE TEAM

Your Team — All Season Long

The standings of hockey teams are listed on the sports pages of the newspaper all season long. The standings will show you which team is in first place, second place, etc., right down to last place.

Some of the abbreviations you'll become familiar with are: GP for games played; W for wins; L for losses; OT for overtime losses; PTS for points; A for assists; G for goals.

Check the standings on the same day of every month and copy down what they say about your team. By keeping track of your team this way you'll be able to see when it was playing well and when it wasn't.

	GP	W	L	OT	PTS
NOVEMBER 1					
DECEMBER 1					
JANUARY 1					
FEBRUARY 1					
MARCH 1					
APRIL 1					
MAY 1					

Final Standings

At the end of the season print the final record of your team below.

YOUR TEAM	GP	W	L	OT	PTS

Your Favorite Players' Scoring Records

While you're keeping track of your favorite team during the season, you can also follow the progress of your favorite players. Just fill in their point totals on the same day of every month.

player	nov 1	dec 1	jan 1	feb 1	mar 1	apr 1	may 1

Your Favorite Goaltenders' Records

You can keep track of your favorite goaltenders' averages during the season. Just fill in the information below.

GAA is the abbreviation for Goals-Against Average. That's the average number of goals given up by a goaltender during a game over the course of the season.

player	nov 1	dec 1	jan 1	feb 1	mar 1	apr 1	may 1

From as far back as he can remember, Niklas Backstrom saw himself as a hockey player. Growing up, Niklas would tell his teachers that he was going to play in the NHL one day. "I never thought of anything else," he recalls with a smile.

But Niklas almost gave up on his dream.

"It hasn't been an easy ride for me to get here. Sometimes it's been very tough," says Niklas. "In my early twenties the dream started to fade away. But then I had a couple of good seasons in Finland, and I started to dream about it again."

"There was a time in my first season when I just decided to go out there and have fun. You never know when you're going to get a chance to play in this league again."

Niklas grew up in Finland, playing mainly in the club system of one of the local teams, HFK Helsinki. Eventually he played for one of the top organizations in the Finnish league, Karpat Oulu. While there, his team's goalie coach encouraged him to switch from playing a stand-up style of goaltending to a butterfly style, which improved his game immensely. He led his team to league championships in 2004 and 2005 and then followed that with a league-best 32 wins in 51 games in 2005–06. His spectacular play caught the attention of Doug Risebrough, who was the general manager of the Minnesota Wild. He took a chance and signed Niklas to a one-year contract.

"If I knew then what I know now, I wouldn't have signed him to a one-year deal," recalls Risebrough.

In his first season Niklas played in 41 games, finishing with a 23–8–6 record and a league-best 1.97 goals-against average. Niklas shared the William Jennings Trophy (best team goals-against average during the regular season) with fellow Wild netminder Manny Fernandez.

By the end of just his first season, Niklas hadn't just established himself as the starting goalie with the Wild, but as one of the best goalies in the entire league. He was finally living his dream.

HOCKEY MEMORY

In 2003–04 Niklas was named Finnish SM-liiga Goaltender of the Year and Playoff MVP after he battled back from a knee injury to lead Karpat Oulu to a championship.

DID YOU KNOW?

Goaltending seems to be a family thing: Niklas' grandfather played in the Finnish professional league for several years, and his father played goal for a junior hockey club.

2008–2009 Stats

GP	W	L	OT	GAA	SO
71	37	24	8	2.33	8

Signed as a free agent by the Minnesota Wild on June 1, 2006

1st NHL Team, Season: Minnesota Wild, 2006–2007

Born: February 13, 1978, in Helsinki, Finland

Position: Goaltender

Catches: Left

Height: 1.85 m (6'1")

Weight: 89 kg (196 lbs.)

DAN BOYLE

It's been a great run so far for Dan Boyle — but certainly not an easy one. Despite a great college career at Miami of Ohio University (he was a finalist for the Hobey Baker Award as the top player in U.S. college hockey in his senior season), he was never drafted. Scouts thought he was too small to be an NHL defenseman. But Dan never let his size stop him. "If a puck goes into the corner, I don't care if I'm going in there with a guy who is 6'6", 250, I'm going to find a way to come out with it."

Dan signed as a free agent with the Florida Panthers in 1998 and spent most of the next two seasons playing in the minors. It was tough at times, but he didn't let his confidence waver.

"You need to be strong and to believe in yourself," says Dan.

"Honestly, I just go out there every shift as if it's my last. I just want to try and make something happen and try and help this team win hockey games."

In 2002 the Panthers traded Dan to Tampa Bay. Two seasons later, his hockey dreams came true as he lifted the Stanley Cup over his head as part of Tampa's 2004 championship. However, in 2007, an off-ice injury to his wrist limited him to only 37 games. Then, unexpectedly, Tampa Bay traded him to the San Jose Sharks. But that has turned out to be a great move for Dan and the Sharks. Boyle was the top-scoring defenseman on a great Sharks team last season — putting up 16 goals and 41 assists for 57 points.

"He's one of those guys who makes everyone better when they're on the ice with him," says Dan's teammate and usual defensive partner Brad Lukowich.

Lukowich's comments are a fitting tribute to a player who spent so many years trying to make himself better and now is able to help get the best out of other players.

So much for being "too small" to be an NHL defenseman.

HOCKEY MEMORY

Dan's most memorable hockey moment was, of course, winning his first Stanley Cup with Tampa Bay in 2004. "I just want to enjoy this for as long as I can," said Dan after the win.

DID YOU KNOW?

While he was in Tampa Bay, Dan hosted a weekly radio show: "Boyle's Blue Line." It was one of the top-rated shows on the station. "I was sort of the locker room DJ, so that's how the idea for the show started."

2008–2009 Stats

GP	G	A	PTS	PIM
77	16	41	57	52

Signed as a free agent by the Florida Panthers on March 30, 1998

1st NHL Team, Season: Florida Panthers, 1998–1999

Born: July 12, 1976, in Ottawa, Ontario

Position: Defense

Shoots: Right

Height: 1.80 m (5'11")

Weight: 86 kg (190 lbs.)

MARTIN BRODEUR

Sometimes life can be more thrilling than fiction. Just look at Martin Brodeur's story: last year, Martin missed 50 games due to an elbow injury just as he was coming close to tying the record for career wins set by Patrick Roy. When he returned in March, in just his eighth game back, Martin tied the record (551) in Montreal — his boyhood home — in front of dozens of friends and family, against the team he grew up worshipping. A couple of nights later he set the record in New Jersey — on St. Patrick's Day.

"Martin is the gold standard of goaltending," said NHL Commissioner Gary Bettman following Martin's record-breaking game. "He is the model of character, consistency and commitment to the craft. He's a champion and a winner above all."

"It's all about winning . . . I have been fortunate to play on great teams and this number will be associated with me for the rest of my life."

Time ticked down in the record-setting game and suddenly, the scale of the accomplishment hit Marty. He had more wins than any other NHL goalie — more than Roy, more than Terry Sawchuck, more than Jacques Plante — all giants of the game.

"It's kind of hard for any athlete to think he's going to be able to get a record like that, especially for goaltending," said Martin after the game. "I think this is what the ultimate record is . . . having the most wins. I never thought that it was going to be possible, but definitely along the way, getting closer and closer, I knew it was going to happen eventually."

It's not as though Marty is anywhere close to being finished. He's 37 as he heads into his 16th NHL season; still hungry to add to his three Stanley Cup wins and his Olympic Gold Medal. He is under contract with the Devils through the 2011–12 season, which gives him more than enough time to write a few more pages for one of hockey's greatest stories.

HOCKEY MEMORY

In 1995, at the age of 23, Marty won his first Stanley Cup. He recalls that the last minute of the clinching game against Detroit "was probably the best minute of my life."

DID YOU KNOW?

Martin and his father, Denis, who was also a goalie, are the only father and son to have ever won medals at the Winter Olympics.

2008–2009 Stats

GP	W	L	OT	GAA	SO
31	19	9	3	2.41	5

New Jersey Devils' 1st choice, 20th overall, in the 1990 NHL Entry Draft

1st NHL Team, Season: New Jersey Devils, 1993–1994

Born: May 6, 1972, in Montreal, Quebec

Position: Goaltender

Catches: Left

Height: 1.88 m (6'2")

Weight: 98 kg (215 lbs.)

JEFF CARTER

Jeff Carter always believed that he could be a big scorer in the NHL, but it took a few seasons for him to get there. Last year was his breakout year as he battled Alex Ovechkin for the NHL goal-scoring crown, finishing with a career high of 46.

"I always knew that I could score," says Jeff. "I think that this year I just started to play with more confidence right from the start of the season."

Another thing he did — and it sounds simple enough — was to shoot more.

"When I was growing up, my Dad always told me that you can't score if you don't shoot. So I always try to put it on net every chance I get," he says.

"I sense that when he gets the puck, people are on the edge of their seats because something special is going to happen."
— Philadelphia general manager Paul Holmgren

It's been quite a while since the Flyers have had a sniper in their lineup. The last time a Philadelphia player topped the league in goals was 1975–76 when Reggie Leach finished with 61 goals. Jeff still has a way to go before he reaches Leach's numbers, but he certainly has the tools. One of his biggest weapons is his shot — it's as hard as they come. He also has a very quick release, making it harder for a goalie to judge where the shot is going.

"His shot is the hardest I've seen in my life," says Philly goalie Antero Niittymaki. "He uses a longer stick than most guys, and he's a big guy too, so his shot is pretty tough to face."

Jeff has also gained weight and gotten stronger since his first couple of years in the league. That has definitely helped his ability to drive toward the net and hold off opposing defensemen. Now, entering his fifth season, he ranks as one of the top goal-scorers in the NHL — right where always believed he could be.

HOCKEY MEMORIES

Before he had set foot in the NHL, Jeff had already been part of two gold medals with Canada at the World Junior Championships and an American Hockey League title with the Philadelphia Phantoms.

DID YOU KNOW?

During the 2007–08 season, when Jeff was coming to the end of his NHL rookie contract and would have been a restricted free agent, the Flyers came close to dealing him to the Vancouver Canucks for Ryan Kesler or to the Toronto Maple Leafs for Tomas Kaberle.

2008–2009 Stats

GP	G	A	PTS	PIM
82	46	38	84	68

Philadelphia Flyers' 1st choice, 11th overall, in the 2003 NHL Entry Draft
1st NHL Team, Season: Philadelphia Flyers, 2005–2006
Born: January 1, 1985, in London, Ontario
Position: Center
Shoots: Right
Height: 1.90 m (6'3")
Weight: 91 kg (200 lbs.)

SIDNEY CROSBY

At the start of last season, there weren't many people who could have predicted that the big offensive star on the Penguins would be Evgeni Malkin rather than Sidney Crosby. It's not that Sidney had a bad season. Far from it. His total of 103 points was still well beyond the dreams of most NHL players. But throughout the season, Sidney struggled to find wingers — aside from Malkin — who could click with him. But the Penguins' general manager, as well as its coaching staff, couldn't find wingers who could bring out the best of Sidney's amazing playmaking ability. From the start of the season, coach Michel Therrien was faced with the dilemma of either putting his two best players on the same line, or splitting them up. He split them up, hoping that the club could have two pretty good lines instead of one

> "There's no doubt, if you're not going to do your job on the ice, it's pretty hard to get the guys to follow you. So, first and foremost, that's what you have to do. Get the job done on the ice."

great one. But Malkin meshed well with Petr Sykora on his line, while Sid had to adjust to the various combinations Therrien (and later, interim coach Dan Bylsma) tried to put together. Sidney, showing the class he's become known for, tried to stay out of the controversy as best he could.

"It's not up to me to decide who I play with and who I don't," Sidney told a group of reporters after a practice. "I can't dwell on it. My job is to create things out there, and I have to try to do that job no matter what."

It will be interesting to watch Sidney and the Penguins this season as they defend their championship. Will the coach decide to reunite Sidney and Malkin? If he does decide to keep them on separate lines, will there be another winger who can create the kind of magic with Sid that Malkin did a couple of seasons ago? Whatever the case, Pittsburgh fans are hoping for a few more points from Sidney, and of course, another Stanley Cup.

HOCKEY MEMORY

Accepting his first Stanley Cup was exactly what Sidney thought it would be like. "It's a dream come true. It's everything you imagined and more."

DID YOU KNOW?

Crosby is the youngest player in NHL history to hit the 100 and 200 career-point marks. Last June he also became the youngest captain to accept the Stanley Cup.

2008–2009 Stats

GP	G	A	PTS	PIM
77	33	70	103	76

Pittsburgh Penguins' 1st choice, 1st overall, in the 2005 NHL Entry Draft
1st NHL Team, Season: Pittsburgh Penguins, 2005–2006
Born: August 7, 1987, in Cole Harbour, Nova Scotia
Position: Center
Shoots: Left
Height: 1.80 m (5'11")
Weight: 91 kg (200 lbs.)

Jarome Iginla

It was March 1, 2009, and 19,000 fans at Calgary's Pengrowth Saddledome stood and cheered as Jarome Iginla turned and nodded to the crowd with his typical modesty. There was plenty to cheer about that night: Jarome had just become the Calgary Flames' all-time points leader, passing Theoren Fleury's mark of 830 career points. On the same night, he also scored his 400th NHL goal and, to top it off, he was the best player on the ice, picking up five points. But this night didn't have a storybook ending. The Flames didn't win the game in come-from-behind fashion — they lost to Tampa Bay 8–6. But it was a night to remember.

"When you start out, you just want to prove to people that you can play in the league," said Jarome after the record-setting game. "You don't think about nights like this."

> "The one word I would say about Jarome Iginla is 'consistency.' He brings his A-game every single night. Very few players can do that."
> — Toronto Maple Leafs general manager Brian Burke

It was inevitable that Jarome would one day hold the title of points-leader for the team. He's been with the Flames his entire career and has never played fewer than 70 games in a season. In an era where most players expect to play with three or four clubs during their career, Jarome is heading into his 13th season wearing the red, white and gold.

And Jarome has long since proven that he can play. He's won the goal-scoring title, the scoring title and the Lester B. Pearson Award as the NHL's most valuable player as voted by his peers. There's just one thing left: the Cup.

The Cup is proving to be elusive for Calgary. Last season they were knocked out by Chicago in the first round. But Calgary fans are hopeful. They still have wonderful memories of the team's 1989 Stanley Cup Championship and the Flames' brilliant run to the Final in 2004. And with superstars like Miikka Kiprusoff and Jarome Iginla in the lineup, there is good reason for that optimism.

HOCKEY MEMORIES

Jarome has great memories of success representing Canada. He's won a World Junior Championship (1996), a World Championship (1997), Olympic Gold Medal (2002) and the World Cup of Hockey (2004).

DID YOU KNOW?

Like many NHL players, Jarome likes to raise money for good causes. He donates $2000 to KidSport for every goal that he scores — that's $170,000 he's raised in the last two seasons!

2008–2009 Stats

GP	G	A	PTS	PIM
82	35	54	89	37

Dallas Stars' 1st choice, 11th overall, in the 1995 NHL Entry Draft
1st NHL Team, Season: Calgary Flames, 1995–1996 playoffs
Born: July 1, 1977, in Edmonton, Alberta
Position: Right Wing
Shoots: Right
Height: 1.85 m (6'1")
Weight: 94 kg (207 lbs.)

MIIKKA KIPRUSOFF

Miikka Kiprusoff fell just short of getting his 50 wins last season. But he certainly made things exciting before finishing with 45 and establishing a club record.

"Fifty wouldn't be out of the realm of possibility," said Flames coach Mike Keenan about midway through last season. "There was a time when scoring 50 goals seemed unachievable, but standards change."

No NHL goalie has ever won 50 games in a season. It has stood, over the years, as the unachievable mark for a goaltender. The great Martin Brodeur — who has accomplished pretty much everything that is possible to achieve as an NHL goalie — came close in 2006–07 when he won 48 games.

> "Sure, there are great physical demands on a goaltender. But I think the greatest demands are on their focus and their mental concentration level."
> — former Calgary coach Mike Keenan on the demands placed on Miikka

Last season Kipper got off to his traditional slow start, but by the time late January rolled around, the 50-win total seemed within reach. He won his 34th game of the season on February 19 and then got five more wins in his next five starts. On March 12 he won his 40th of the season — the record, although in sight, was going to be tough to achieve with just a month to go. When asked about it, he preferred to focus on the team.

"You start to go crazy if you think too much about that sort of thing," Miikka told reporters during the chase. "It's a team game; it's all about winning. Of course, after the season, you look at your numbers and you can see how well you played, but right now it's about the team."

Miikka only picked up five more wins over his last 13 starts. Some say he was tired — he played in 76 games and faced over 2,100 shots. But his total of 45 wins was still the best in the NHL last season. And you can count on him taking another run at 50 again this season.

HOCKEY MEMORY

Miikka's greatest NHL memory was the 2003–04 NHL season. He won the Vezina Trophy and then helped lead the Flames to the Stanley Cup Final. They lost to Tampa Bay in seven games, but Miikka was spectacular — playing in 26 playoff games and picking up 5 shutouts.

DID YOU KNOW?

Miikka's older brother, Marko, played parts of two NHL seasons with Montreal and the New York Islanders.

2008–2009 Stats

GP	W	L	OT	GAA	SO
76	45	24	5	2.84	4

San Jose Sharks' 5th choice, 116th overall, in the 1995 NHL Entry Draft
1st NHL Team, Season: San Jose Sharks, 2000–2001
Born: October 26, 1976, in Turku, Finland
Position: Goaltender
Catches: Left
Height: 1.85 m (6'1")
Weight: 83 kg (184 lbs.)

ALEX KOVALEV

There have been several occasions during his career when Alex Kovalev has had to battle. He has sometimes disagreed with coaches wanting him to play a style that he felt didn't suit his game. He's battled through slumps and injuries. But, in the end, Alex has had a successful career. He's been a professional hockey player since he was 16 years old and in the NHL since 1992.

There were many who had written the Russian superstar off after the 2006–07 season, when he only managed 18 goals and 29 assists. But the following season Alex was on Montreal's top line and enjoyed his best season since his career year of 2001 with Pittsburgh. He led Montreal in scoring with 35 goals and 49 assists for 84 points. But then last year both Alex and the team struggled. Alex was as puzzled by the team's hardships as anyone.

> "He's the best stickhandler I've ever seen. Quickness. Hands. He's a much better stickhandler than me. He's got the talent to be the best player in the world."
> — former teammate Mario Lemieux

"I came out this year and felt pretty good, so I felt like I could do a little bit extra," says Alex. "But it was time to go back and try not to do everything by yourself, and use your partners a little bit."

There was also an element of bad luck. Even his coach at the time, Guy Carbonneau, noted that he was "creating the most scoring chances, but he seemed to be hitting a crossbar, or hitting a defenseman or something like that."

But Alex, as he has many times during his great career, battled on. While he didn't have the type of season he did in 2007–08, he was still one of Montreal's top players, finishing with 26 goals and 39 assists for 65 points. If the past is anything to go by, Alex will be back on form this season. He has never been one to quit when the going gets tough. That's what makes him a superstar.

HOCKEY MEMORY

Alex loved playing in his first NHL All-Star Game in 2001. "I was really excited. I took pictures of everybody, no matter who it was."

DID YOU KNOW?

Alex is a licensed pilot. He's logged over 1000 hours of flight time and flown more than a dozen different types of aircraft, including helicopters.

2008–2009 Stats

GP	G	A	PTS	PIM
78	26	39	65	74

New York Rangers' 1st choice, 15th overall, in the 1991 NHL Entry Draft

1st NHL Team, Season: New York Rangers, 1992–1993

Born: February 24, 1973, in Togliatti, USSR (now Russia)

Position: Right Wing

Shoots: Left

Height: 1.89 m (6'2")

Weight: 102 kg (224 lbs.)

NICKLAS LIDSTROM

Nicklas Lidstrom has been reaching one milestone after another the last few seasons, and he will reach yet another major milestone early this season: he won't be very far into this NHL season before he reaches the 1,000 career-point mark. He will become only the second Swedish-born player to ever scale those heights (Mats Sundin was the first). In 2006 Nick became the first European-born captain of the Detroit Red Wings and, in June 2008, he became the first European-born captain to accept the Stanley Cup on behalf of his team.

"It was and always will be something special being the first European captain to win it," says Nick. "There was a time when you didn't see many European captains in the league, and it was a special feeling to be the first one [to accept the Cup]."

> **"I think I'll appreciate all of the honors when I'm done playing. When you're in the middle of everything, you just get ready for the next game. You can't relax and think too much of the past."**
> **— Nick talking about approaching career milestones**

There haven't been many players as consistent as Nick over the last 20 years — since joining the team in 1991–92 he's missed few games. He's also won the Norris Trophy as the NHL's top defenseman six times and been named to the First All-Star Team nine times.

And Detroit has been just as consistent: the Wings have never missed the playoffs in his time with the club (Detroit actually hasn't missed the playoffs since 1989–90); they have made it to the Stanley Cup Final six times and won it four; last season they became only the fourth team in NHL history to record four consecutive 50-win seasons; and during Nick's entire time with the club, they've had only two captains — Nick and Steve Yzerman.

"I learned a lot by watching Stevie being captain for 15 years while I was playing with him," says Nick. "One of the biggest things was . . . to earn the respect of your teammates."

As Nick hits the 1,000 career-point milestone, it's obvious that he has the respect of teammates and opponents alike.

HOCKEY MEMORY

As part of the Stanley Cup tradition, each player on the winning team gets to spend a day with it. One of the first things Nick did with his day was to take it back to the rink where he learned to play as a kid in Vasteras, Sweden.

DID YOU KNOW?

Nick has played 1,331 games since the start of his 17-season career. No other player in NHL history has played that many games, in the same number of seasons, from the start of his career.

2008–2009 Stats

GP	G	A	PTS	PIM
78	16	43	59	30

Detroit Red Wings' 3rd choice, 53rd overall, in the 1989 NHL Entry Draft
1st NHL Team, Season: Detroit Red Wings, 1991–1992
Born: April 28, 1970, in Vasteras, Sweden
Position: Defense
Shoots: Left
Height: 1.85 m (6'1")
Weight: 86 kg (189 lbs.)

EVGENI MALKIN

Heading into last season, Evgeni Malkin had an unusual problem: he needed to follow up his impressive 2007–2008 season with the Penguins. But how to do any better? In just his second season, Evgeni had stepped up and filled the gaping hole left in the roster after Sidney Crosby was injured early on. At the end of the season, Evgeni led the team in scoring, finishing second in the league to Alex Ovechkin.

But great hockey players thrive on challenges. Evgeni tore it up right out of the gate last season. By mid-November he was wrapping up a 13-game point-scoring streak (6 goals, 21 assists, for 27 points) and proving to teammates and opponents alike that he was always improving.

> **"I'm not the best. Sid [Crosby] is the best. [Alex] Ovechkin is the best. Sid makes good passes all the time. It's easy to play with Sid."**

"You can see it, the confidence is just pouring out of him," said Calgary Flames defenseman Anders Eriksson early last season. "The guy can do it all — soft hands, good shot and a great ability to read the game as well."

That confidence has helped Evgeni to his greatest season yet. He won the Art Ross Trophy as the NHL's leading scorer with 113 points and then, a few weeks later, he became the first Russian to win the Conn Smythe and hoisted the Stanley Cup over his head.

Evgeni also greatly improved his English skills. Hockey fans sometimes don't understand the importance of this, but imagine you've moved to a country where you can't understand what people are saying, or read signs or books or even watch TV, all while trying to establish yourself in the best hockey league in the world. It can all be pretty intimidating.

But Evgeni hasn't gotten to where he is by not responding to expectations and pressure. Whether he's doing his talking on the ice by scoring or off the ice as he learns English, the message is the same: there aren't many challenges this superstar won't answer.

HOCKEY MEMORY

You would have to guess that last season's performance would be the number one hockey memory for Evgeni. But his rookie season wasn't bad either. In 2006–2007 he became the first player in 89 years to score at least one goal in each of his first six NHL games.

DID YOU KNOW?

In 2006, Evgeni pulled off the rare feat of playing in the World Junior Championships, the Winter Olympics and the World Championships in the same year.

2008–2009 Stats

GP	G	A	PTS	PIM
82	35	78	113	80

Pittsburgh Penguins' 1st choice, 2nd overall, in the 2004 NHL Entry Draft

1st NHL Team, Season: Pittsburgh Penguins, 2006–2007

Born: July 31, 1986, in Magnitogorsk, Russia

Position: Center

Shoots: Left

Height: 1.9 m (6'3")

Weight: 88 kg (195 lbs.)

ZACH PARISE

Zach Parise knows he doesn't score "highlight goals" — the types of goals that someone like Sidney Crosby scores, where a player beats another with a deke, speeds past two others, fakes the goalie one way and then goes the other and puts the puck in the top corner. Those goals are fantastic, but not nearly as common as the type of goals Zach tends to score.

"I don't score the highlight reel goals. They come from hard work," Zach says. "I like to get in the corners, get a little dirty, really work for it. It's kind of an old-fashioned goal, I guess."

> **"Zach's got the gift . . . not only is he a very competitive player, he's got everything else that goes with it."**
> **— New Jersey head coach Brent Sutter**

Hard work has served Zach well during his career, but he also has the other tools that you need to build something special. When you watch him play, you notice right away that he's a player who's always able to get into the open. He reads the ice extremely well. Zach has taken Wayne Gretzky's motto, "Go to where the puck is going to be" to heart; he'll suddenly appear in an open spot, take a feed from a teammate and create a scoring chance. He also has an incredibly good shot and what players refer to as "soft hands" for giving and taking passes.

Zach has built on his few years in the league. In his rookie season he watched his older teammates and absorbed all he could. The next year he stepped things up and scored 31 goals, followed by another 30-goal season. Then last season, his best yet, he led the team with 8 game-winning goals and 14 power-play goals. He also led the Devils in scoring with 94 points, and in goal-scoring with 45. Zach approached franchise records in both of those categories, just missing out on becoming the first New Jersey Devil to score 50 goals and record 100 points in a season. So, while he may not score many highlight-reel goals, Zach will happily take the ones that come from hard work as he continues to be one of the top forwards in the NHL.

HOCKEY MEMORY

Zach's dad, J.P. Parise, played 13 seasons in the NHL with 5 different clubs. People who remember his father say that Zach's style of play reminds them of his dad's.

DID YOU KNOW?

Zach played his first NHL game against Sidney Crosby, who was also playing his first NHL game that night. Crosby went goalless while Zach scored on his first career shot-on-goal.

2008–2009 Stats

GP	G	A	PTS	PIM
82	45	49	94	24

New Jersey Devils' 1st
choice, 17th overall, in
the 2003 NHL Entry Draft
1st NHL Team, Season:
New Jersey Devils,
2005–2006
Born: July 28, 1984, in
Minneapolis, Minnesota
Position: Left Wing
Shoots: Left
Height: 1.80 m (5'11")
Weight: 86 kg (190 lbs.)

MARC SAVARD

Looking just at stats, you might think that Boston's Marc Savard has lost just a little bit of his offensive touch the last couple of seasons. In 2005–06 and 2006–07, Marc finished just shy of 100 points (97 points in 2005–06 and 96 in 2006–07). His totals the last couple of seasons have been slightly short of those two great years, with 78 points in 2007–08 and 88 last season. But any hockey fan will tell you that scoring stats never tell the entire story. Marc's defensive game has improved over the past couple of seasons. Just look at his plus/minus rating — in 2005–06 he was –19, but last season he was +25.

"When I came here to Boston, [Boston head coach] Claude Julien helped me to develop that part of my game," says Marc. "I know better what to do down low or in our end. I think I play better away from the puck now than I used to."

"Not only being able to say something, but being able to go out and do it."
— Marc's take on what makes a good leader

It's not as though Marc's offensive game has suffered as a result of him paying attention to defensive responsibilities. He's still the top offensive player on the Bruins and one of the best in the league. Mark has led the Bruins in scoring for the last three seasons. He was also one of their top offensive gunners in the playoffs last season — especially in the Bruins'

first-round victory over Montreal, as he racked up four points in one game.

"I find Savvy skating more this year than he has in the past," says Julien. "He's involved in plays at both ends of the ice and that's helped his game to grow."

Heading into this season, Marc is a more complete player than he's ever been. He may score a little less than he used to, but the trade-off of a few goals and assists in order to help his club play better defensively has been a good one.

HOCKEY MEMORY

As a pro, Marc will never forget his first Stanley Cup playoff game in 2008 with the Boston Bruins against the Montreal Canadiens. With good reason — he had to wait 10 seasons (659 games) before he got his chance in the post season.

DID YOU KNOW?

Marc is an avid golfer and he'd love to play on the PGA Tour once his playing days are over. In 2005, he got a taste of a tour event when he caddied for his friend, PGA veteran Stewart Cink.

2008–2009 Stats

GP	G	A	PTS	PIM
82	25	63	88	70

New York Rangers' 3rd choice, 91st overall, in the 1995 NHL Entry Draft
1st NHL Team, Season: New York Rangers, 1997–1998
Born: July 17, 1977, in Ottawa, Ontario
Position: Center
Shoots: Left
Height: 1.78 m (5'10")
Weight: 87 kg (191 lbs.)

SHELDON SOURAY

When the Edmonton Oilers signed Sheldon Souray as a free agent in July 2007, it seemed like a perfect match. Sheldon was just breaking out as an NHL defenseman, coming off a career-best 64-point season with Montreal. The signing was also a homecoming of sorts for the native of Elk Point, Alberta. Sheldon grew up cheering for the great Oilers teams of the late 1980s.

"Once the Oilers got into the mix it became a pretty easy decision to make," says Sheldon about his signing. "My heart was really into it. Just the thought of putting on the uniform got me excited."

> "It's hard. He has such an easy motion. Even when you know it's coming, you have a clear look at him, you think you see the puck, and then it's by you."
> — Calgary goalie Miikka Kiprusoff on Sheldon's shot

However, Sheldon suffered a shoulder injury in October during a game against Vancouver and, eventually, had to have season-ending surgery in February. So, in his first season with the Oilers, Sheldon got just 3 goals and 7 assists for 10 points. Hardly the great homecoming Sheldon or the Oilers had hoped for.

"Unfortunately the fans didn't get to see much of me on the ice that first year because I spent most of it rehabbing in the trainer's room," recalls Sheldon.

But the veteran resolved to come back and show fans and teammates why the Oilers had decided to give him $27 million over five years. Sheldon bounced back last season and was the top-scoring defenseman on the team with 23 goals and 30 assists for 53 points, and was one of the top-ten defensemen in the league.

After failing to make the playoffs last season, Sheldon and the Oilers are determined to make the grade this season. He has as much desire as ever to keep chasing his dream of success with the team he grew up worshipping.

HOCKEY MEMORY

Sheldon remembers the ball cap that he had when he was a kid cheering for the Oilers. It was signed by superstar Jari Kurri. "No one else could touch it," he says.

DID YOU KNOW?

During the Oilers' SuperSkills competition last season, Sheldon fired a slap shot at 106.7 mph (171.7 km/h) and set the unofficial NHL record for hardest shot.

2008–2009 Stats

GP	G	A	PTS	PIM
81	23	30	53	98

New Jersey Devils' 3rd choice, 71st overall, in the 1994 NHL Entry Draft
1st NHL Team, Season: New Jersey Devils, 1997–1998
Born: July 13, 1976, in Elk Point, Alberta
Position: Defense
Shoots: Left
Height: 1.93 m (6'4")
Weight: 106 kg (233 lbs.)

MARK STREIT

In 1999 Mark Streit left his home country of Switzerland with the hope of making it in the NHL. He managed to earn a spot on the Utah Grizzlies of the East Coast Hockey League — not the big step he had hoped for. But he did finish the season with the Springfield Indians of the American Hockey League, which inched him closer toward his goal. The following season, however, he decided to return to Switzerland.

Mark never gave up, though; his game matured and improved and he eventually caught the eye of the Montreal Canadiens. The Habs made Mark a late pick (262nd overall) in the 2004 Entry Draft. He was 26 years old and one of the oldest players ever drafted by an NHL club, but his dream was still alive.

> "I think he's made a big statement this year, not just being one of the top defensemen but a well-rounded defenseman. He's been reliable defensively and usually goes against the other team's top two lines and kills penalties."
> — Islanders' Head Coach Scott Gordon

A couple of seasons later, Mark made his NHL debut at the age of 28 — old by professional hockey standards. And in 2007–08 Mark truly broke out, having his best season and leading Montreal defensemen with 62 points.

"It took me a while, and I have to thank Montreal for being patient and giving me the time to develop," says Mark. "Every year was a bit better and I had more confidence."

Surprisingly, the Habs didn't re-sign Mark after his breakout season. He became an unrestricted free agent and signed a five-year deal with the New York Islanders. A bad move for Montreal; a great move for the Islanders.

When Mark returned to Montreal for the NHL All-Star Game last season, he felt a big sense of accomplishment.

"It was an unbelievable honor," says Mark. "Not just for me, but for Swiss hockey."

Most would say there was a lot more hard work involved than luck.

HOCKEY MEMORY

Mark has been a big part of Switzerland's National Team, playing for the team in the last 11 World Championships and also at the Olympics in 2002 and 2006. He was the captain of the 2006 team in Turin that reached the quarterfinals after shocking both the Czech Republic and Canada in the round robin.

DID YOU KNOW?

When Mark signed his deal with the Islanders, he became the second-highest paid Swiss professional athlete. At the top of the list is tennis great Roger Federer.

2008–2009 Stats

GP	G	A	PTS	PIM
74	16	40	56	62

Montreal Canadiens' 8th choice, 262nd overall, in the 2004 NHL Entry Draft

1st NHL Team, Season: Montreal Canadiens, 2005–2006

Born: December 11, 1977, in Englisberg, Switzerland

Position: Defense

Shoots: Left

Height: 1.83 m (6')

Weight: 89 kg (197 lbs.)

JOE THORNTON

It's tough not to love a player like Joe Thornton. Even if you're not a San Jose Sharks fan, and even if he's playing well against your favorite team, you still have to respect Joe's amazing work ethic. There must be nights when he's tired, battered and bruised. But he's always there, pulling on his jersey and playing his best.

"You wake up and you're lying in bed sore and you think you can't go," says Joe. "But you go to the rink and you loosen up and get treatments from the trainer. You know your body pretty good and you've got to hop on things before they become a big problem."

Joe hasn't missed a regular season game since he was traded to the San Jose Sharks on November 30, 2005. Heading into this season, the consecutive games streak stands at 304 games. But what's amazing is that Joe plays the game hard — taking as much physical punishment as he gives.

"When he's out there throwing passes you have to be at your best at all times because he'll find you. When you think he won't find you, he'll put the puck on your stick. My first two NHL goals were great passes [from Joe] from behind the net."
— San Jose teammate Devin Setoguchi

Although Joe works hard to stay in shape and is aware of any small aches and pains, he also has a passion for the game which helps drive a streak like his.

"For Joe, hockey isn't just a job, it's fun," says Sharks coach Todd McLellan.

This season promises to be a challenging one for Joe. He'll be trying to lead the Sharks to the top in the Western Conference again, and he'll also be hoping to help Canada win a gold medal at the Winter Olympics in Vancouver. And through it all, you'll be able to count on a couple of things: Joe will do his best not to miss a game, and he'll give it his all every time he's on the ice. He wouldn't have it any other way.

HOCKEY MEMORY

Joe's earliest hockey memories are of playing on the rink in the backyard with his father and brothers. He says the best part about growing up in St. Thomas, Ontario, was being able to play the game on outdoor rinks.

DID YOU KNOW?

Joe has had many good coaches during his career, but he credits Mike Keenan with "turning on a switch" while he was coaching him in Boston, putting him on the road to becoming the player he is now.

2008–2009 Stats

GP	G	A	PTS	PIM
82	25	61	86	56

Boston Bruins' 1st choice, 1st overall, in the 1997 NHL Entry Draft
1st NHL Team, Season: Boston Bruins, 1997–1998
Born: July 2, 1979, in London, Ontario
Position: Center
Shoots: Left
Height: 1.93 m (6'4")
Weight: 107 kg (235 lbs.)

JONATHAN TOEWS

You have to be a special kind of player to be named a team captain at just 20 years old. Usually it's an honor given to someone who has been in the league for a few years. But before the start of last season, the Blackhawks named Jonathan the 34th captain in the history of the franchise, making him the third-youngest captain in NHL history.

"Why is John the captain?" says Chicago Head Coach Joel Quenneville. "Because . . . he's a special person and a special player."

Jonathan was the third overall pick in 2006, and Chicago scouts hoped he could develop into a franchise player for a team that was badly in need of success. Long gone were the days of full houses and playoff heroics. People in Chicago just didn't care about the Blackhawks anymore.

"I think a lot of being a leader is just being an influential person and not kind of hiding in the corner. And when things have to be said you stand up and say them and kind of express yourself for what you think is right."

But people took notice of Jonathan after he scored in his very first NHL game. He finished his rookie season with 24 goals and 30 assists for 54 points and was runner-up to his teammate Patrick Kane for the Calder Trophy as the NHL's rookie of the year. He followed that up last season with 34 goals, 35 assists for 69 points, and helped Chicago step into the playoffs for the

first time since 2002.

There are those who say Jonathan is a big reason interest in hockey has made a resurgence in Chicago. Seats are full again and people around town are once again talking about the Hawks, especially after their surprising trip to the Western Conference Final last May.

"You know, it's a lot of fun for us to walk down the street or go into restaurants and hear people talking about the Hawks," says Jonathan.

They're definitely talking about them, and they're also talking about their young captain. For the first time in a long time, the Blackhawks look like they're on the right track.

HOCKEY MEMORY

Jonathan remembers playing a lot of shinny on his family's backyard rink in Winnipeg, Manitoba. He used to play a lot with his younger brother David, who was drafted by the New York Islanders in 2008.

DID YOU KNOW?

Phoenix Coyotes veteran Shane Doan helped prepare Jonathan for his entry into the NHL. The two were teammates on Team Canada at the 2007 World Hockey Championship.

2008–2009 Stats

GP	G	A	PTS	PIM
82	34	35	69	51

Chicago Blackhawks' 1st choice, 3rd overall, in the 2006 NHL Entry Draft

1st NHL Team, Season: Chicago Blackhawks, 2007–2008

Born: April 29, 1988, in Winnipeg, Manitoba

Position: Center

Shoots: Left

Height: 1.88 m (6'2")

Weight: 96 kg (211 lbs.)

REFEREE SIGNALS

Do you know what is happening when the referee stops play and makes a penalty call? If you don't, then you're missing an important part of the game. The referee can call different penalties that result in anything from playing a man short for two minutes to having a player kicked out of the game.

Here are some of the most common referee signals. Now you'll know what penalties are being called against your team.

Boarding
Checking an opponent into the boards in a violent way.

Cross-checking
Striking an opponent with the stick, while both hands are on the stick and both arms are extended.

Charging
Checking an opponent in a violent way as a result of skating or charging at him.

Elbowing
Checking an opponent with an elbow.

High-sticking
Striking an opponent with the stick, which is held above shoulder height.

Holding
Holding back an opponent with the hands or arms.

Hooking
Using the blade of the stick to hold back an opponent.

Icing
Shooting the puck across the opposing team's goal line from one's own side of the rink. Called only if the opposing player touches the puck first.

Interference
Holding back an opponent who does not have the puck in play.

Kneeing
Using a knee to hold back an opponent.

Misconduct
A ten-minute penalty — the longest type called. Usually for abuse of an official.

Roughing
Shoving or striking an opponent.

REFEREE SIGNALS

Slashing
Using the stick to strike an opponent.

Spearing
Poking an opponent with the blade of the stick.

Slow whistle
The official waits to blow his whistle because of a delayed offside or delayed penalty call. Done while the opposing team has control of the puck.

Tripping
Tripping an opponent with the stick, a hand or a foot.

Unsportsmanlike conduct
Showing poor sportsmanship toward an opponent. For example: biting, pulling hair, etc.

Wash-out
Goal not allowed.

FINAL TEAM STANDINGS 2008–2009

EASTERN CONFERENCE

Atlantic Division

Team	GP	W	L	OT	PTS
NEW JERSEY	82	51	27	4	106
PITTSBURGH	82	45	28	9	99
PHILADELPHIA	82	44	27	11	99
NY RANGERS	82	43	30	9	95
NY ISLANDERS	82	26	47	9	61

Northeast Division

Team	GP	W	L	OT	PTS
BOSTON	82	53	19	10	116
MONTREAL	82	41	30	11	93
BUFFALO	82	41	32	9	91
OTTAWA	82	36	35	11	83
TORONTO	82	34	35	13	81

Southeast Division

Team	GP	W	L	OT	PTS
WASHINGTON	82	50	24	8	108
CAROLINA	82	45	30	7	97
FLORIDA	82	41	30	11	93
ATLANTA	82	35	41	6	76
TAMPA BAY	82	24	40	18	66

WESTERN CONFERENCE

Central Division

Team	GP	W	L	OT	PTS
DETROIT	82	51	21	10	112
CHICAGO	82	46	24	12	104
ST. LOUIS	82	41	31	10	92
COLUMBUS	82	41	31	10	92
NASHVILLE	82	40	34	8	88

Northwest Division

Team	GP	W	L	OT	PTS
VANCOUVER	82	45	27	10	100
CALGARY	82	46	30	6	98
MINNESOTA	82	40	33	9	89
EDMONTON	82	38	35	9	85
COLORADO	82	32	45	5	69

Pacific Division

Team	GP	W	L	OT	PTS
SAN JOSE	82	53	18	11	117
ANAHEIM	82	42	33	7	91
DALLAS	82	36	35	11	83
PHOENIX	82	36	39	7	79
LOS ANGELES	82	34	37	11	79

GP = Games played; W = Wins; L = Losses; OT = Overtime; PTS = Points

TOP TEN POINTS LEADERS 2008–2009

	PLAYER	TEAM	GP	G	A	P	S	S%
1	EVGENI MALKIN	PITTSBURGH	82	35	78	113	290	12.1
2	ALEX OVECHKIN	WASHINGTON	79	56	54	110	528	10.6
3	SIDNEY CROSBY	PITTSBURGH	77	33	70	103	238	13.9
4	PAVEL DATSYUK	DETROIT	81	32	65	97	248	12.9
5	ZACH PARISE	NEW JERSEY	82	45	49	94	364	12.4
6	ILYA KOVALCHUK	ATLANTA	79	43	48	91	275	15.6
7	RYAN GETZLAF	ANAHEIM	81	25	66	91	227	11.0
8	JAROME IGINLA	CALGARY	82	35	54	89	289	12.1
9	MARC SAVARD	BOSTON	82	25	63	88	213	11.7
10	NICKLAS BACKSTROM	WASHINGTON	82	22	66	88	174	12.6

GP = Games played; G = Goals; A = Assists; P = Points;
S = Shots; S% = Percentage

TOP TEN GOALIES — TOTAL WINS 2008–2009

	PLAYER	TEAM	GP	W	L	OT	SA%	GA	GAA
1	MIIKKA KIPRUSOFF	CALGARY	76	45	24	5	.903	209	2.84
2	EVGENI NABOKOV	SAN JOSE	62	41	12	8	.910	150	2.44
3	CAM WARD	CAROLINA	68	39	23	5	.916	160	2.44
4	HENRIK LUNDQVIST	NY RANGERS	70	38	25	7	.916	168	2.43
5	NIKLAS BACKSTROM	MINNESOTA	71	37	24	8	.923	159	2.33
6	TIM THOMAS	BOSTON	54	36	11	7	.933	114	2.10
7	MARC-ANDRE FLEURY	PITTSBURGH	62	35	18	7	.912	162	2.67
8	RYAN MILLER	BUFFALO	59	34	18	6	.918	145	2.53
9	STEVE MASON	COLUMBUS	61	33	20	7	.916	140	2.29
10	ROBERTO LUONGO	VANCOUVER	54	33	13	7	.920	124	2.34

GP = Games played; W = Wins; L = Losses; OT = Overtime and/or Shut-Out Losses;
SA% = Save percentage; GA = Goals Against; GAA = Goals-Against Average

END-OF-SEASON STATS

Countdown to the Cup 2009–2010

EASTERN CONFERENCE

CUP
FINAL

CONFERENCE
FINAL

CONFERENCE
SEMI-FINALS

CONFERENCE
QUARTER-FINALS

THE CHAMPION:

WESTERN CONFERENCE

CONFERENCE FINAL

CONFERENCE SEMI-FINALS

CONFERENCE QUARTER-FINALS

NHL AWARDS

Here are some of the major NHL awards for individual players. Fill in your selection for each award and then fill in the name of the actual winner of the trophy.

HART MEMORIAL TROPHY

Awarded to the player judged to be the most valuable to his team. Selected by the Professional Hockey Writers Association.

2009 winner: **Alex Ovechkin**

Your choice for 2010: _____

The winner: _____

ART ROSS TROPHY

Awarded to the player who leads the league in scoring points at the end of the regular season.

2009 winner: **Evgeni Malkin**

Your choice for 2010: _____

The winner: _____

CALDER MEMORIAL TROPHY

Awarded to the player selected as the most proficient in his first year of competition in the NHL. Selected by the Professional Hockey Writers Association.

2009 winner: **Steve Mason**

Your choice for 2010: _____

The winner: _____

JAMES NORRIS TROPHY

Awarded to the defense player who demonstrates throughout his season the greatest all-round ability. Selected by the Professional Hockey Writers Association.

2009 winner: **Zdeno Chara**

Your choice for 2010: _____

The winner: _____

VEZINA TROPHY

Awarded to the goalkeeper judged to be the best. Selected by the NHL general managers.

2009 winner: **Tim Thomas**

Your choice for 2010: _____

The winner: _____

MAURICE RICHARD TROPHY

Awarded to the player who scores the highest number of regular-season goals.

2009 winner: **Alex Ovechkin**

Your choice for 2010: _____

The winner: _____

WILLIAM M. JENNINGS TROPHY

Awarded to the goalkeeper(s) who played a minimum of 25 games for the team with the fewest goals scored against it.

2009 winners: **Tim Thomas and Manny Fernandez**

Your choice for 2010: _____

The winner: _____

LADY BYNG MEMORIAL TROPHY

Awarded to the player judged to have exhibited the best sportsmanship combined with a high standard of playing ability. Selected by the Professional Hockey Writers Association.

2009 winner: **Pavel Datsyuk**

Your choice for 2010: _____

The winner: _____

FRANK J. SELKE TROPHY

Awarded to the forward who best excels in the defensive aspects of the game. Selected by the Professional Hockey Writers Association.

2009 winner: **Pavel Datsyuk**

Your choice for 2010: _____

The winner: _____

CONN SMYTHE TROPHY

Awarded to the player most valuable to his team in the Stanley Cup Playoffs. Selected by the Professional Hockey Writers Association.

2009 winner: **Evgeni Malkin**

Your choice for 2010: _____

The winner: _____

BILL MASTERTON MEMORIAL TROPHY

Awarded to the player who best exemplifies the qualitites of perseverance, sportsmanship and dedication to hockey. Selected by the Professional Hockey Writers Association.

2009 winner: **Steve Sullivan**

Your choice for 2010: _____

The winner: _____

Dedicated to the memory of former NHL player Peter Zezel.
Peter was proudly featured in Hockey Superstars 1992-93,
and is sadly missed by all who knew him and watched him
play the game he loved so much. Rest in peace.

— P. R.

Illustrations by Bill Dickson

ISBN-10 0-545-985374 / ISBN-13 978-0-545-98537-6

6 5 4 3 2 1   Printed in Canada   09 10 11 12 13